BATTLE OF BRITAIN

BATTLE OF BRITAIN

Norman Franks

BISON GROUP

First published in 1990
Bison Books Ltd
Kimbolton House
117A Fulham Road
London SW3 6RL

ISBN 0-86124-584-9

Printed in Hong Kong

10 9 8 7 6 5 4 3 2 1

PAGES 2-3: *A painting by Paul
Nash depicting dogfights over the
Thames Estuary (August-October
1940).*

PAGE 5: *Members of an antiaircraft
battery enjoy a meal break while
their comrades blast away at a
formation of German bombers.*

CONTENTS

1
BRITAIN ALONE

Britain was alone. The debris of Dunkirk had disappeared and those soldiers who were still in France were either dead or in prison camps. Western Europe was now under the heel of the German jackboot.

In an astonishingly short space of time France, Belgium and Holland had fallen to the Germans' lightning attack – their now famous Blitzkrieg tactic. In that time the British Army had been forced out of France, the Royal Air Force had been overwhelmed, and Britain's allies had been defeated and forced to surrender their arms and their countries. In one month Hitler's forces, already victors in Poland and Norway, had achieved what the Kaiser's armies had failed to do in the four years between 1914-18.

Anyone standing on the south coast of England in mid-June 1940, and looking out across the English Channel toward France could feel tangibly that he and his country were alone. True, Britain still had her Commonwealth, but although some of its fighting men were in the Mother country, Canada, South Africa, Australia, New Zealand and so on were too far away to be of any real help. They could send more men and supplies but that was all. Britain was still alone and it was obvious to everyone that the Germans' next conquest must be the British Isles. In their way stood Air Chief Marshal Hugh Dowding, Commander in Chief of the RAF's Fighter Command, and his fighter pilots.

Britain's natural defense was, and has always been, the Channel. Although the advent of the airplane had in one sense made Britain less of an island, an invading army had still to cross this watery barrier. That could only be achieved, again because of the airplane, if the invaders had mastery of the air.

To gain this mastery over the English Channel and southern England, the German Luftwaffe needed to defeat the Royal Air Force, or more especially, its Fighter Command. In mid-June 1940 Fighter Command was in poor shape by comparison with the attackers. Losses over Dunkirk and in the Battle of France had seen to that. It is said that one can prove anything with figures and various accounts of comparative strengths of the RAF and the Luftwaffe do differ.

The Luftwaffe, under the command of Hermann Wilhelm Goering, a former fighter pilot of World War I, had been building its strength for a number of years. By August 1938 it had nearly 3000 aircraft, and the total had increased to 3750 by the time Poland was attacked on 1 September 1939, which plunged the world into World War II. Despite losses sustained in Poland, and later over Norway in April 1940, the Luftwaffe mustered nearly 5000 aircraft by May 1940. Of this total 3900 were in the two air groups, *Luftflotte* 2 and *Luftflotte* 3, which were poised to lead the Blitzkrieg in the West.

Although the air forces of France, Belgium and Holland could field a large number of fighting aircraft, the RAF in France had only four squadrons of Hawker Hurricanes and two of Gloster Gladiator fighters during the period known as the 'Phony War' – September 1939-May 1940. When the Germans invaded France and the

LEFT: *Weary members of the British Expeditionary Force arrive at a port in southeast England. With the fall of France, Britain stood alone, its security resting with the Royal Navy and the Royal Air Force.*

ABOVE RIGHT: *Air Chief Marshal Hugh Dowding, the main architect of RAF Fighter Command's victory during the Battle of Britain.*

PREVIOUS PAGES: *A picture taken from the Luftwaffe magazine* Der Adler, *showing a Bf 109E fighter parked on an airfield in northern France.*

RIGHT: *Pilots of the RAF's No 1 Squadron scramble during the Battle for France. The RAF lost over 1000 aircraft during the fighting, as well as many of its trained pilots.*

Low Countries on 10 May, reinforcements of RAF aircraft were sent to France but in 10 days it was obvious that there was no stopping the German advance. The RAF gave a good account of itself in France, its pilots fighting themselves to a standstill. Yet finally those who survived had to be evacuated back to England. It was because of Hugh Dowding that Britain's fighter force had not been completely whittled away in the French campaign.

A scheme approved in 1935 promised Fighter Command a minimum of 53 squadrons by 1939 with which to defend the British Isles. In 1936, when Dowding became commander in chief, he only had 15 regular and three auxiliary squadrons. This was increased to only 24 regular and six auxiliary units by 1938 – and every one was equipped with a variety of outdated biplanes.

When the German offensive began on 10 May 1940, the RAF had 2750 frontline aircraft, of which just over 1000 were fighter types. In the first two days of the offensive four more fighter squadrons were sent across to France and on the 13th a further 32 Hurricanes and pilots flew over. Dowding had now been forced to commit around a third of his fighter force to France. Clearly this could not continue if he was to retain sufficient fighters to defend Britain.

He put his case forward forcibly at a Cabinet meeting, illustrating with graphs that if the present rate of attrition continued for a further two weeks the RAF would not have a single Hurricane left in France – or Britain! He followed this with his now famous and courageous

Fighter Command had to defend all of Britain, not just the south, although it was anticipated that the main assault would take place in that region.

Those in command viewed the coming battle with a good deal of foreboding. The task of defending Britain with such a small force against a victorious Luftwaffe was daunting. The pilots who would fight the battle viewed the coming struggle in a variety of ways. Some who had been in France felt utterly devastated at being on the losing end; a few even felt that Britain too must fall. Others were keen to hit back, to have another go. Many others, having tasted action above Dunkirk, were equally eager to have another crack at the Germans. Those pilots still to see action were, in the main, raring to go. Yet by far the majority believed they would prevail – defeat was unthinkable. This was perhaps a testament of youth, for most of Britain's fighter pilots were young. However young, they were the professionals, led by professionals. The wartime trainee pilots were not in evidence in any great number as yet. Whatever thoughts went through their minds, everyone was keen to 'get stuck in.' Yet within a few short weeks, those who were still alive were physically and mentally exhausted and any excuse for a rest was gratefully taken. If rain or bad weather stopped flying it was a godsend. However, as July began each one of them stood ready to play his part in the forthcoming battle.

letter to the Under Secretary of State for Air, setting out his fears and asking for the Air Ministry to commit itself as to what it considered the level of strength needed to defend Britain. This in itself won him few friends in high places but it eventually did the trick. Shortly afterward came the order from Winston Churchill that no more fighters would leave the UK, whatever France's need.

The Royal Air Force eventually lost over 1000 airplanes in France and Norway, half of which were fighters. This represented two-thirds of all aircraft delivered to the RAF since the war began. Even more serious was the loss of so many valuable aircrew, both regular air force men and peacetime trainees. Their loss was not in vain for not only did they inflict considerable damage on the Luftwaffe, thereby reducing the number of aircraft which would eventually be used against Britain, but those who survived to return to Britain had gained immeasurable experience. The Dunkirk evacuation cost the RAF 100 fighters and about 80 pilots, leaving Fighter Command with roughly 470 serviceable aircraft by early June, of which just 330 were Hawker Hurricanes and Supermarine Spitfires. There were only 36 more in immediate reserve.

A month later, the first week in July, with both sides about ready to meet each other in deadly action, *Luftflotte* 2 and *Luftflotte* 3 numbered 2075 aircraft, of which 900 were fighters, 875 bombers and 300 dive bombers. *Luftflotte* 5, based in Norway, threatened the eastern side of England and Scotland and had 123 bombers and 34 twin-engined fighters. The RAF at this moment had just 46 fighter squadrons plus two equipped with Defiants (soon to be relegated to night fighting only) with four more squadrons in course of formation. The total number of aircraft was between 600-700 with 1253 pilots – 197 short of establishment. With this number,

LEFT: *Boulton Paul Defiants of the RAF's No 264 Squadron in flight. Without forward-firing armament, these aircraft suffered grievous losses at the hands of the Luftwaffe.*

RIGHT: *A British radar station, one of many that provided invaluable intelligence during the battle. The three towers on the left acted as transmitters of information; those on the right gathered vital data on the Luftwaffe's sorties.*

BELOW LEFT: *Former leader of von Richthofen's 'Flying Circus' in World War I, Hermann Goering commanded the Luftwaffe throughout World War II.*

BELOW: *The operations room of RAF Bentley Priory, control center of the RAF's Fighter Command.*

One asset that the defenders had was Britain's integrated radar system, which was far in advance of the Germans' own development. When the battle started it gave the fighter pilots early warning of the approach of flying raiders, an estimate of their number and, with a degree of accuracy, their height. With help from the Observer Corps, 30,000 civilian volunteers, Britain had a good chance of knowing where the enemy was coming from and where he was heading.

Although as yet the air force had little chance to test its fighter defenses in nine months of war, the success in intercepting those few raiders that had made flights over Britain was encouraging. It was a practiced art and one that had been practiced often enough. This was due to the energies of the leader of Fighter Command, Hugh Dowding. His devotion to the concept of total defense of his country brought success although often his approach did not help his subsequent career. Even

RIGHT: *Members of the Royal Observer Corps scan the skies for formations of German aircraft. Using relatively unsophisticated equipment they were able to plot the height, strength and direction of the Luftwaffe's raiders.*

BELOW: *Air Vice-Marshal Trafford Leigh-Mallory, a veteran of World War I, led the RAF's 12 Group, covering central England, during the battle.*

to his pilots he was an aloof figure – only later would they appreciate his great qualities of leadership.

Dowding's principal air leaders were the three group commanders whose squadrons would bear the brunt of the coming attack. All three had served in the air force in World War I. In the southeast of England was 11 Group, commanded by Air Vice-Marshal Keith Park, a New Zealander. North of the River Thames, covering most of Essex, Suffolk and Norfolk, was 12 Group, controlled by Air Vice-Marshal Trafford Leigh-Mallory. Air Vice-Marshal Sir Christopher Quintin Brand, a South African, commanded 10 Group in the southwest.

Opposing them was Reichsmarschal Hermann Goering and his three main air group commanders. *Luftflotte* 2 was led by Generalfeldmarschal Albrecht Kesselring, a soldier turned airman, while *Luftflotte* 3 was headed by Generalfeldmarschal Hugo Sperrle. Sperrle had commanded the Condor Legion during the Spanish Civil War, where the German had gained considerable experience fighting for General Franco's forces. *Luftflotte* 5 in Norway was under the command of Generaloberst Hans-Jurgen Stumpf, a former staff officer.

Historians have conveniently divided the Battle of Britain into five phases although at the time, to the ordinary fighter pilot, there seemed to be a general buildup from about 10 July, as the Luftwaffe stepped up its attacks, until October/November when they began to cease.

As July began, the RAF was still licking its wounds after the French and Dunkirk campaigns. Dowding's strength was far from 100 percent; several units had lost much of their equipment in France and were not fully operational. The Luftwaffe had moved rapidly into bases in Belgium, Holland and northern France, had been reinforced from Germany and now stood ready to take the offensive against Britain. By mid-July Luft-

waffe strength was in the region of 2000 aircraft. Keith Park's 11 Group had just 190 or so day fighters and as it was the RAF's most vulnerable sector, the odds against it were considerable.

The RAF's main antagonists in the battle were Heinkel 111, Dornier 17 and Junkers 88 bombers, Junkers 87 'Stuka' dive bombers and Messerschmitt 109 and 110 fighters. All had had their successes in Poland, Norway and France, but over Britain their shortcomings soon became evident. The three bombers were all twin-engined craft with relatively short ranges when fully laden. In daylight raids they were vulnerable to fighter attacks and close escort by fighters proved essential as the battle progressed. The Ju 87, while successful in the Blitzkrieg type of action when it could accurately blast a path for advancing ground troops, quickly proved extremely vulnerable in actions over southern England and had to be withdrawn from major involvement by mid-August. The Messerschmitt Bf 109E single-seat fighter was a dangerous adversary for RAF pilots, but it was hampered by its short range. Often it had only a short time in the combat zone, usually measured in minutes, and its pilots were ever mindful of their fuel levels. The twin-engined, two-seat Bf 110 was also dangerous but it had already proved vulnerable in combat over France. Pilots often had to resort to flying in defensive circles when under attack, thus leaving the bombers open to attacks by British fighters.

The Luftwaffe was organized principally for use as a direct support of an advancing land army. It was, therefore, totally unsuited to an offensive war involving distances such as France to Britain.

Both fighters and bombers were equipped with the 7.9mm machine gun, roughly equivalent to the RAF's Browning .303inch machine gun, but in addition the Messerschmitts carried 20mm cannons which were

BELOW: *Three Spitfires take off to intercept a formation of German bombers somewhere over southeast England.*

who had collided with a Heinkel 111 over the sea. Six RAF fighters had been damaged.

The battles over the coastal convoys were vicious and costly to both sides. Several young, inexperienced pilots were lost chancing their arm against the Luftwaffe, some chasing Germans back toward France, only to be jumped by Messerschmitt 109s over the sea.

Over a convoy on the 12th, Dorniers and Heinkels of 11/KG2 and 111/KG53 were intercepted by Hurricanes of 17, 85, 151 and 242 Squadrons from Martlesham, Debden, Coltishall and North Weald. One pilot in 17 Squadron, Flying Officer Count M B Czernin, spotted 12 Heinkel 111s coming in fast from the east at 8000 feet. He immediately went into a climbing turn to the left, then, stick over and a kick on the left rudder and he was plunging down to attack. The station commander at North Weald, Wing Commander F V Beamish, flying with 151 Squadron, was also on hand. Attacking three Dorniers, he was:

'. . . met by heavy crossfire with much tracer. After a long burst at the left hand Dornier, his port engine blew up and stopped, his undercarriage dropped down and he broke away from the formation.'

Meanwhile, Czernin and one of his section, Pilot Officer D H W Hanson, had broken off the first action and followed Beamish's attack on the three Dorniers. They attacked the leading bomber and sent it into the sea. Its pilot was the Staffelkapitan of KG3, Hauptmann Machetski.

Later in the day three pilots of 74 Squadron took off to investigate a raid plotted 15 miles northeast of Margate. They saw antiaircraft fire, coming from a ship, exploding around a single Heinkel 111. The section leader, Flight Lieutenant A G Malan, DFC, opened fire with his machine guns from 300 yards and silenced the rear gunner of the bomber, allowing his two wingmen to finish it off.

RIGHT: *An English Channel convoy under attack during the initial stages of the Battle of Britain.*

BELOW: *Hurricanes of the RAF's No 85 Squadron on patrol. Slower than the Luftwaffe's Bf 109 fighters, Hurricanes were deployed against bomber formations; enemy fighters were left to the faster and more maneuverable Spitfires.*

Sailor Malan was again in evidence on 28 July when he and his men tangled with Werner Mölder's JG51. No 74 Squadron was using Manston as a base and had been scrambled at 1350 hours when a raid had been reported approaching Dover. Malan's Spitfires went after the Messerschmitt escort, but the bombers turned away. The Spitfire pilots attacked the Bf 109s; no less than three were destroyed and three others were damaged. One of those damaged was flown by Mölders himself.

Malan reported the action:

'. . . turned on to their tails without being observed and led Red Section into the attack. Gave one enemy aircraft two-second bursts from 250 to 100 yards. He attempted no evasion tactics except a gentle right-hand turn and decreasing speed, by which I concluded he had at least had his controls hit (shot away). I then turned on to another 109 which had turned past my nose and I delivered three deflection bursts at 100 yards. He went down in a spiral.'

Verband	Auftrag	Start	Landug.	
		13. 7. 40.		
I/54	Portsmouth	6⁰⁰	7¹⁰	20 Ju 88
II/54		6⁰⁵		16 Ju 88
K.G.54		6³⁷		He 111 Seeno...
K.G.54		7⁰⁶		1 He 111 "

LEFT: *A Luftwaffe controller records the details of several sorties by Ju 88s and He 111s against Portsmouth.*

BELOW LEFT: *Captured by the nose-camera of a Luftwaffe fighter, a group of Spitfires endures the effects of a strafing run.*

The squadrons that periodically used RAF Manston as a forward base were constantly in the front line. Little wonder that this southeastern tip of England was soon called 'Hellfire Corner' by the pilots. It became liberally pitted with bomb craters as low-flying Bf 109s were easily able to slip in to fly a strafing run over the base. Rochford (Southend) was another airfield and forward base similar to Manston and also used by squadrons from Hornchurch.

At Manston the pilots occupied a dispersal site on the far side of the airfield. They had some huts for both ground personnel and aircrew during readiness periods. This sometimes caused delays in bringing food and refreshments to dispersal as it was a long way from the domestic amenities of the camp. It was code named 'Charlie 3.' The typical routine for Manston, Rochford (and some others) was: Readiness at dawn. Takeoff straight away to fly a convoy patrol. Refuel and return to immediate readiness until mid- or late afternoon taking part in whatever sorties might come along. Then back to the parent station, remaining at readiness until finally released at dusk.

No 65 Squadron used Rochford during one period. The conditions were somewhat primitive. Their Spitfires were parked into the wind while the pilots used an old civilian clubhouse as flight hut, restroom and eating place. There they would wait for the call for action. Parked outside the clubhouse was a 15-hundredweight Bedford truck and a motorbike which was used to get to the aircraft in a hurry when the call came.

In the clubhouse was a single telephone which was answered by whoever was sitting nearest to it, while everyone else made for the door at top speed, aiming for the truck. 'Thumbs up' and away they went, leaving the chap on the phone to get the whole message then follow on the motorbike and pass on the message as they climbed away on takeoff. 'Thumbs down' stopped the panic and everyone settled down again.

One morning a young pilot named Paddy Finucane was nearest the phone and his sign sent everyone aboard the truck and away. As the pilots took to the air they looked down to see Finucane get on to the bike, fall off and try to climb back from the other side. With obvious signs of panic he jumped up and down as the others flew off without him. Upon landing it was discovered that Finucane could not ride a motorbike nor drive a car. They never let Finucane sit by the telephone after that.

The telephone became the center of attention in many crew rooms, dispersal huts and pilots' caravans over those summer months of 1940. The pilots would try to ignore its presence but as soon as it rang, their hearts missed a beat. Its message could send them racing to their waiting fighters, or it could be just an innocuous

message, perhaps from the canteen, asking how many lunches were required, or the station commander wanting to speak to the commanding officer. The scenes at Manston and Rochford were repeated on a score or more fighter bases in southern England where the fighter pilots waited for the call for action.

As July gave way to August so too came the change of tactics by the Luftwaffe. The time of probing was at an end. If Hitler had any intention of invading Britain he had to attack in the summer, and before he did, Fighter Command had to be destroyed. On 19 July Hitler made his 'last appeal to reason' speech to the Reichstag – but he should have known Britain would in no way contemplate surrender. Hitler was confident of victory, for

in his hands was the latest intelligence report comparing the Luftwaffe strength with that of the RAF. In its conclusion it showed that the Luftwaffe was clearly superior to the RAF in strength, equipment, training and command. In the event of intensive air warfare the Luftwaffe would be in a position to achieve a decisive effect in 1940 in order to support an invasion. What the report did not allow for was the dogged, stubborn attitude of the British in general, or the skilled determination of the pilots who stood in the way of outright German victory.

The first phase of the battle ended after the first week in August. In that phase the Luftwaffe lost nearly 200 aircraft, about twice as many as the Royal Air Force.

ABOVE: *An enduring image of the Battle of Britain: RAF pilots run toward their Spitfires at the beginning of a scramble.*

RIGHT: *A Bf 109 from Stab III, Jagdgeschwader 26, which crash-landed near Margate on 24 July, the victim of a Spitfire from No 65 Squadron.*

The second phase of the battle began on 8 August. The Luftwaffe now saw its task as mainly a fighter-versus-fighter conflict in order to destroy the British fighter force. The bombers which attacked British targets, mainly airfields, provided the bait to bring the Hurricanes and Spitfires to battle; then the Bf 109 pilots could deal with them.

At the start of August there was a lull in Luftwaffe activity and it was clear to Dowding and to Keith Park that this had to mean that the enemy was regrouping ready for a massive all-out assault. Whether or not Hitler really meant to invade Britain, there can be little doubt that everyone in Britain did expect him to do so. Therefore, every pilot knew that destiny lay very much in his hands.

In the German intelligence appreciation of the RAF referred to above, the Luftwaffe underestimated the strength of the RAF fighters by half! This was to lead to various complications within the German High Command and the continuing shortcomings of intelligence reports led to much frustration among German aircrew who continued to meet strong resistance when they had been told that the RAF had been practically wiped out.

Dowding was a little more confident at this stage, for trained pilots were quickly making up the recent losses and he had now more than 1400 pilots; his only dilemma was that they lacked experience. Nearly 100 experienced regular squadron and flight commanders had been lost since May.

Of the many air actions which occurred on the 8th, two flown by Pilot Officer A N C Weir of 145 Squadron produced three victories. During the first part of the morning he shot down a Bf 109 and a Ju 87. In a lunch-time battle he got another Bf 109:

'Saw 110s in two groups five miles apart, flying in defensive circles low down. Three Hurricanes at 12,000 feet circled, wondering the best way to attack and asking for help. After ten minutes decided to dive when a 109 flew across in front of me – a decoy I thought. Pulled round to get on its tail and we flew round in circles till I was just gaining a position from which I could fire. He dived steeply and I fired from astern from 500 yards.'

Another pilot saw the Bf 109 crash into the sea.

Goering had promised Hitler that his Luftwaffe would clear the sky of the RAF in readiness for invasion during early August. Now that his fliers had built up their strength, they were ready to go. His strength was 2250 serviceable aircraft between Cherbourg and Norway. Against this Dowding had 708 aircraft, an increase in the number he had started the battle with owing to the tremendous effort by aircraft factory workers.

As far as the Luftwaffe was concerned, the Battle of Britain began on 8 August and Goering, head of the mightiest air force in the world, set 10 August as the date for his major assault, his *Adlertag* ('Eagle Day'). However, bad weather forced a postponement.

On the 11th raids were directed against Portland, while a diversionary attack was mounted in the area of Dover. Three RAF squadrons went up to engage the Dover attack while seven were scrambled to patrol Weymouth, near Portland. These found 150 German aircraft, Ju 88s and He 111s escorted by Bf 109s and Bf 110s. Huge dogfights began as the bombers pressed home attacks against the docks, oil tanks, gasworks and army barracks. At the end of the day the Germans had lost 38 aircraft but the RAF lost 32 precious fighters.

PREVIOUS PAGES: *Groundcrew refuel and rearm a trio of Hurricanes of No 601 Squadron at Tangmere airfield, near Portsmouth. The pilot (far left) is Max Aitken, son of newspaper magnate Lord Beaverbrook.*

LEFT: *Leading Luftwaffe ace Werner Mölders (second from left) recounts a dogfight over southeast England to three of his colleagues.*

RIGHT: *Curious members of the public study the remains of a Bf 109 from JG52 before it is put on display, May 1941.*

BELOW: *The victor and the vanquished. A pilot poses by the nose of a Ju 88. The state of the aircraft suggests that souvenir hunters have been at work.*

The next day was equally hard for the RAF defenders, as raids were directed against Portsmouth, radar stations and coastal airfields. The arithmetic was a little better. Some 31 Germans were shot down for 22 RAF fighters, although the Germans claimed 70 Spitfires and Hurricanes destroyed. These exaggerated claims did little to help German intelligence reporting to the Luftwaffe High Command. The claims included the total destruction of one Spitfire squadron at Manston – 65 Squadron. They had been taxying out for takeoff when Dorniers of KG2 bombed the base, but most of them got off amid bomb bursts to join in the battle above.

RAF Hawkinge was also badly hit. Two hangars and the station workshops were destroyed and the stores building was damaged. Twenty-eight bomb craters pit-

LEFT: *Injured Luftwaffe crewmen arrive at London's Victoria station under armed escort on their way to a prisoner of war camp.*

RIGHT: *A group portrait of Spitfire pilots from No 74 Squadron based at RAF Manston. The airfield, one of the most heavily attacked during the battle, came under the jurisdiction of Keith Park's 11 Group.*

BELOW: *A group photograph of pilots from Spitfire-equipped No 611 Squadron.*

BELOW RIGHT: *D M Crook served as a pilot officer with No 609 Squadron and downed a Stuka during a dogfight over Lyme Bay on Adlertag (Eagle Day), 13 August 1940. He was credited with eight kills during the battle.*

ted the airfield but it was operational next morning. The next morning was Eagle Day – 13 August.

The Germans were still not fully aware of how the operational structure of RAF Fighter Command worked, a fact borne out by the many attacks against airfields not even used by the defending fighter force. They were also unaware as to how the reporting chain from radar stations was coordinated. Their reconnaissance flight interpretation made some astonishing revelations, most of which were totally inaccurate.

Eagle Day saw heavy attacks on Eastchurch airfield in the morning and against Portland, Southampton and

ing
the
and
ash

/
bet
jus
alt
ate
RA

airfields in Hampshire and Kent during the afternoon. It was a massive effort; 1485 sorties were flown by the Luftwaffe crews, the highest number to date. B Flight of 65 Squadron scrambled from Manston at 1530 hours and off Dover they spotted 20 Bf 109s. One of the pilots engaged was Pilot Officer B E Finucane:

P/O D.M. CROOK. D.F.C.   609 SQUADRON

'Saw three 109s flying in formation . . . and attacked number three, firing fairly long bursts from 300 to 75 yards. 109 burst into flames and dived into the clouds. I then spotted a lone 109 climbing up 400 yards ahead. Closed to 200 yards and gave it a burst. Drawing near could see the 109 had orange wing tips. 109 half rolled very slowly and seemed to shudder then slowly spin away. . . .'

Pilot Officer P C F 'Paddy' Stevenson of 74 Squadron was flying as Number Two to Sailor Malan and saw a Bf 109 chase after his leader:

'He must have thought I was a Bf 109 but when he suddenly dived away I followed him and gave a two-second deflection burst. The EA (enemy aircraft) lurched slightly and went into a vertical dive. I saw the EA dive straight into the sea 15 miles SE of Dover and disappear in a big splash.'

Stevenson climbed again and was about to engage more Bf 109s when he was hit from behind. Looking back he saw a dozen Bf 109s on his tail, half of whom seemed to be firing at him. His Spitfire was hit and he had to get out as he went into a dive:

'I pulled the hood back. I got my head out of the cockpit and the slipstream tore the rest of me clear out of the machine. My trouser leg and both shoes were torn off. I saw my machine crash into the sea a mile off Deal.'

The pilots of 609 Squadron got in among a formation of Ju 87s over Lyme Bay shortly after 1600 hours and shot down six of them without loss. Pilot Officer D M Crook, Number Three in Blue Section, saw several Bf 109s pass right under his squadron:

'I immediately broke away and attacked one which was behind the rest. Fired a good burst from dead astern. He rocked violently and then turned over and burst into flames and crashed near Hardy's Monument behind Weymouth.'

At the other end of the scale, the Hurricanes of 56 Squadron did not fare so well. They broke through some

battle. Again it was RAF airfields which took the brunt of these assaults.

British radar detected a massive buildup of enemy aircraft all along the enemy coast in the late morning. Then they came. Over 100 headed in toward Hawkinge and Lympne. At 1140 hours Flying Officer A Eyre of 615 Squadron found enemy aircraft over Folkestone:

'Suddenly Blue 3 (Pilot Officer K T Lofts) noticed six 109s behind and above coming out of the sun. Blue 3 got on to the leading 109 and I gave him three bursts of five seconds, attacking from behind, above and below. He burst into flames about 8000 feet and baled out.'

Then in the north a raid was mounted by *Luftflotte* 5, hoping to meet little opposition while the defenders were busy over the south coast. An estimated force of over 30 raiders turned out to be 65 bombers and 34 110s. The attacks were directed against Newcastle and Sunderland in the north, and Driffield farther to the south. The radar had everything under control and far from having an easy time of it, this German force found Spitfires and Hurricanes waiting for them. They lost 16 bombers and seven fighters, and the RAF lost just one Hurricane and one pilot.

In the south Manston was raided again by low-flying Bf 109s which destroyed two parked Spitfires. Then Martlesham was attacked by Stukas and Messerschmitts. At the same time 100 raiders headed in toward Deal, followed by 150 over Folkestone. Seven RAF squadrons intercepted them but the heavy fighter escort kept them occupied. Eastchurch was bombed as were factories at Rochester. Radar sites at Dover, Rye, Bawdsey and Foreness were attacked but without any real success. In the late afternoon some 250 raiders

came in, crossing the coast near the Isle of Wight, spreading raids out over Hampshire and Wiltshire. Middle Wallop, Odiham and Worthy Down airfields were the targets. Eleven RAF squadrons intercepted this force, causing losses totaling 25 for the loss of 11 fighters. Nos 87 and 213 Squadrons up from Exeter engaged part of this raid, finding a huge formation of German aircraft coming in from the south; Ju 87s with Bf 109s and 110s stacked up behind them. No 87 Squadron's commanding officer gave the order to attack and within minutes he was shot down and killed. Three others of the squadron went down in the fight, one pilot was killed, a second was wounded and the third baled out. Flight Lieutenant I R Gleed dived to the attack:

'I dived unseen by EA out of the sun, attacking a 110 which burst into flames. Broke away, climbed and dived for vertical attack on a 110. Starboard engine of 110 caught fire and it broke formation.'

He was then attacked by two Bf 109s:

'They attacked me, one did a head-on attack, the other made for my tail. Got a good burst at engine and underside of head-on 109 then aileron turned vertically downwards.'

At 1815 hours another raid of over 70 aircraft approached Biggin Hill and Kenley but actually bombed West Malling and later Croydon. This was followed by a Bf 110 raid on a factory just south of London near Croydon. Nos 32 and 111 Squadrons intercepted them to shoot down four.

By the end of the day, 182 German aircraft had been claimed by the RAF, with losses of 34 fighters. Actual German losses totaled 75, but it was still a significant

LEFT: *Hurricanes of No 32 Squadron, out of fuel and ammunition, come in to land at Biggin Hill, 15 August 1940. The airman with the flag guides the fighters through the bomb craters that litter the airfield.*

RIGHT: *Pilots of No 17 Squadron's A Flight pose for a photograph at Debden. On cowling, from left to right: D Hanson, W J Harper and G R Bennette; on wing, from left to right: L W Stevens, G E Pitman and G Griffiths.*

BELOW: *A pair of Hurricane Mark Is from No 501 (County of Gloucester) Squadron take off to intercept German aircraft, 16 August 1940.*

BELOW RIGHT: *Victim of a dogfight on 23 August, a Bf 110 goes on public display at Hendon Park. Designed as an escort fighter, the Bf 110 suffered heavy losses in combat against the RAF's more versatile fighters.*

victory. The Germans claimed 101 victories. The day's fighting had been ferocious; the Germans had flown 1786 sorties, the RAF 974. One outcome was that *Luftflotte* 5 made no further major contribution to the battle, its bombers going to *Luftflotte* 2 later in August.

Another was that the Ju 87 and Bf 110 were finally deemed to be inadequate for their allotted tasks. Owing to the bomber losses, the Bf 109 pilots were subsequently not allowed a free rein to combat RAF fighters, being ordered to stay close to the bombers. This was

totally against the purpose for which the Bf 109 had been designed. In future, therefore, they had to await the assaults by Spitfires and Hurricanes rather than seek out their adversaries.

The Luftwaffe's fury continued the next day despite the losses of the 15th. Airfields were once again subjected to attack, while the RAF flung themselves at the raiding aircraft. All remained quiet until an hour before midday when a series of raids was flown over Kent and Norfolk. Manston and West Malling were bombed yet again. Three heavy raids were mounted at midday which made for the Thames Estuary, Dover and Southampton. This split the defending fighters – an estimated 350 German aircraft were reported. Twelve squadrons from 10, 11 and 12 Groups were scrambled to intercept. Tangmere, Gosport, Lee-on-Solent and Brize Norton were all hit but only Tangmere was a fighter field. Flight Lieutenant R F Boyd of 602 Squadron based at Tangmere's satellite base at Westhampnett made what is probably the quickest kill of the battle. Scrambling when Tangmere was being bombed, he ran straight into a Ju 87, shot it down and was back on the ground in less than a minute after takeoff.

These raids cost the Germans a further 45 aircraft, the RAF losing 22 and eight pilots. One of these was the Hurricane flown by Flight Lieutenant J B Nicolson of 249 Squadron. He and his section became embroiled with German raiders over Southampton at 1245 hours. It was Nicolson's first taste of action. Following an abortive chase after three Ju 88s, he and his two wingmen were rejoining the main squadron formation when they were bounced by Bf 109s. All three Hurricanes were hit; one pilot was forced to land at Boscombe, a second baled out only to have his parachute shredded by ground fire, sending him to his death. Nicolson's machine was set ablaze and he was wounded. He heard four big bangs as cannon shells from an attacking Bf 109 hit home:

'The first shell tore through the hood over my cockpit and sent splinters into my left eye. One splinter I discovered later, nearly severed my eyelid. I couldn't see through that eye for blood. The second cannon shell struck my spare petrol tank and set it on fire. The third shell crashed into the cockpit and tore off my right trouser leg. The fourth shell struck the back of my left shoe. It shattered the heel of the shoe and made quite a mess of my left foot.

I was just thinking of jumping out when suddenly a Messerschmitt 110 whizzed under me and got right in my gunsight . . . I pressed the gun button for the Messerschmitt was in nice range; I plugged him first time and could see my tracer bullets entering the German machine.'

Despite the flames he continued to attack until he finally was forced to take to his parachute. Wounded and badly burned he survived to receive Fighter Command's only Victoria Cross of the war.

Hurricanes of 615 Squadron were in evidence during a raid near Brighton at 1615 hours. Pilot Officer J A P McClintock attacked one He 111 he found out of formation. He opened fire from 300 yards closing in to 50. The

LEFT: *An RAF fighter closes in on its prey – a He III. In the days between* Adlertag *and 23 August, the Luftwaffe lost an estimated 300 aircraft.*

BELOW: *The interior of a 'Chain Home' radar station, with its personnel operating receiver equipment.*

BELOW RIGHT: *RAF pilots of No 79 Squadron at Biggin Hill. From left to right: Cartwright, Parker, Joslin (killed in action on 7 July), Stones, Murray and Edwards.*

Heinkel's starboard engine began to pour out smoke, followed by flames, then it went down. Pilot Officer C R Young attacked two others, one of which he left smoking. The second, hit by a long burst, went down into cloud and Young followed it. Coming out he fired again from 100 yards. The bomber leveled out at sea level, streaming smoke, but a third burst sent it crashing into the sea leaving a large green swirl on the water.

Flight Lieutenant P C Hughes, an Australian with 234 Squadron, shot down two Bf 109s at around 1830 hours south of the Isle of Wight. He saw 50 Bf 109s circling above him and led his section in a climbing attack:

'I fired a deflection shot at the nearest 109 . . . it caught fire and blew up. I felt a jolt and turned sharply and found another 109 on my tail. He immediately climbed away in front of me where I shot him behind the cockpit. He caught fire and crashed into the sea. Four Ju 87s went by, heading south. I closed to attack but as I fired my tailplane got shot through by a 109. My aircraft dived and my tabs were shot away.'

The next major assault against RAF airfields came on the 18th. Kenley, Biggin Hill, Croydon and West Malling were all attacked. Some 100 bombs fell on Kenley, destroying four Hurricanes, one Blenheim and three training types. Several hangars were destroyed and there were some personnel casualties. Kenley's 615 Squadron was attacked by Bf 109s at high level. One pilot was lost, another baled out wounded and two more force landed, one being wounded.

Flying Officer F Gruska, a Polish pilot flying with 65 Squadron from Rochford, was reported missing at 1330 hours. His wrecked Spitfire with his body still in the cockpit was recovered from Stodmarsh near Canterbury in July 1975 – 35 years later!

A massed Stuka attack on Ford and Thorney Island airfields was met by 152, 601, 602 and 234 Squadrons. Sixteen of the dive bombers were shot down, six more being damaged, two of which crashed at their base. Eight escorting Bf 109s were also shot down but four Spitfires and two Hurricanes were lost.

Flying Officer W Rhodes-Moorhouse, son of the World War I VC winner, was a flight leader with 601 Squadron, although he often led the squadron in action. He got one of the Bf 109s:

'There were two formations of Ju 87s, 20 machines in each, flying in close vic formation and stepped up in line astern was about 20 Bf 109s above and to the sides. I gave the order for sections to form line astern and turning right I dived on the rear formation of Ju 87s making a head-on attack from the starboard bow. I saw no result from this attack. Passing quickly I became engaged with a lot of Bf 109s at which I fired a number of short bursts . . . only one of these did I see crash as I had no time to follow or watch results of my attack.'

The day was another disaster for the Luftwaffe, 71 of its aircraft failed to get home. Twenty-seven RAF fighters and 10 pilots were lost. The 18th saw the death-knell of the Ju 87 over England, until late autumn at any rate. This made a total of 194 Luftwaffe aircraft lost between 15-18 August, with many more damaged.

Although the RAF was still suffering casualties it was nevertheless making its presence felt. Yet Keith Park was extremely conscious of the dangers his pilots were in and had to try and restrain their exuberance in engaging enemy fighters which in themselves posed no danger to Britain. His fighter strength had to damage the German bombers and stop them turning his fighter bases into rubble.

After the mammoth battles of the last few days there was a relative calm owing to bad weather between 19-23 August. The latter date ended the second phase of the battle which had cost the Luftwaffe in the region of 300 aircraft. The third phase began on the 24th. It was the crucial phase for Fighter Command – the Germans were after its blood – the RAF had to be destroyed.

3
AIRFIELDS ATTACKED

The fighter pilots of the RAF were tiring. The previous weeks had been a hard slog. Pilots in the south of England had already been called to perform Herculean tasks almost daily. Readiness was at dawn – always at dawn. Readiness states varied from cockpit 'standby' of two minutes or readiness in the dispersal hut (or outside it in the sunshine) of five minutes. From time to time the squadron might be put down at 15 or 30 minutes availability, which gave the pilots time to go for a wash or bath or a hot meal.

Pilot Officer H A C Bird-Wilson, a member of 17 Squadron based at Debden for the first two phases of the battle, remembers those moments which began with the telephone ringing at dispersal. Most rings meant 'scramble,' excitement, acceleration of heart beats and a dash to the aircraft. On a dawn scramble it was known for some pilots to scramble in their pajamas. Takeoffs from the grass airfield were usually in squadron strength of four sections of three Hurricanes, from two different corners of the airfield. At times 12 Hurricanes approached each other in the center of the airfield, lifting up over each other. Somehow they got away with it. The climb-out vector was always to the southeast to the left of London. Climbs were always made flat-out and with full throttle. Their ground controllers were superb and information was continually passed to the pilots, such as, enemy formation of 160 plus approaching the south coast at 12,000 feet, and above there are more bandits joining up with them – so climb harder!

It was a strange phenomenon, but many individual squadrons scrambled flew on their own. Each climbed to engage the enemy as just one unit, but hoped that somewhere near would be at least one other 12-man squadron. (Harold Bird-Wilson recalls this feeling vividly.) In contrast, Pilot Officer H M Stephen who flew with 74 Squadron, remembers being too damn scared of his legendary commanding officer, Sailor Malan, to think

of anything else than to climb hard and get stuck into the Germans.

If squadrons engaged alone there would be 12 against 100 or more aircraft. As they fought as small units they

PAGE 34: *Ju 87 Stukas on a sortie. These slow moving dive-bombers, although strikingly successful in Poland and France, suffered heavy losses during the battle and were withdrawn from the action.*

ABOVE: *Pilots Stephen (left) and Mungo-Park of 74 Squadron, a Spitfire-equipped unit.*

LEFT: *The crew of a Heinkel bomber enjoy a meal in the hot summer sun of 1940 before heading out on a mission.*

RIGHT: *An aerial view of Portsmouth harbor under attack. During the afternoon of 26 August 50 German bombers escorted by up to 100 fighters attacked the port causing much damage.*

had little idea of what the overall picture was. They took off, flew hard, fought hard and those who got back waited for the next call. They learned little of what was going on outside their immediate circle of action. They heard the news bulletins, of course, and read newspapers, but it did not mean that much to them. Even their squadron commanders knew little more and they certainly did not know about the whole picture of the battle. The individual pilot merely lived from dawn readiness until released at dusk, and with dawn at 0330 hours or so, it was a long day. Little wonder they slept where they sat or lay between flights.

At their dispersal points the pilots had certain creature comforts. Some had easy chairs, others had camp beds pulled out into the sunshine. There was the inevitable record player and sometimes a radio. Twelve men would sit in the warm sun in a variety of uniform or flying clothing, Mae West life jackets on. Within a short distance stood their aircraft, trolley starter accumulator plugged in. Each fighter's ground crew sitting or lying nearby was ready to start the machine as soon as the yell galvanized their pilots into a run toward them.

Everyone's day started early. If the pilots were ready at dawn then the ground crews were up earlier, testing the engines, running them up and checking them over. Flight sergeants tried to get the most aircraft available

following the previous day's battle damage. Each aircraft would have its daily inspection.

Most pilots were woken up still tired. Their cheery batmen would ignore the rude comments that would greet them as they woke their pilots. Once up those who could concentrate would gulp down mugs of tea before getting themselves down to the flights. They would look over their own aircraft, talk to the ground crew, ensure that their parachute was ready and that the flying helmet was in position, usually draped over the gun sight, ready to be pulled on as they sat in the cockpit and were strapped in by a crewman. Everyone hoped for bad weather but, generally speaking, the summer of 1940 was beautifully warm and sunny.

In the early days, many pilots were physically sick in the early mornings. In 74 Squadron for example, after they had washed, shaved and drunk a cup of tea, they would be off to the airfield. Before reaching dispersal, several of them were sick, usually getting rid of the last of the beer drunk the previous evening. Drinking the odd pint or two helped guarantee a few hours deep sleep – an important consideration. The squadron doctor wondered why this sickness occurred and discovered that being so early in the morning, coupled with nervous tension (this might be their last day on earth), the body's sugar content was low, and breakfast was still

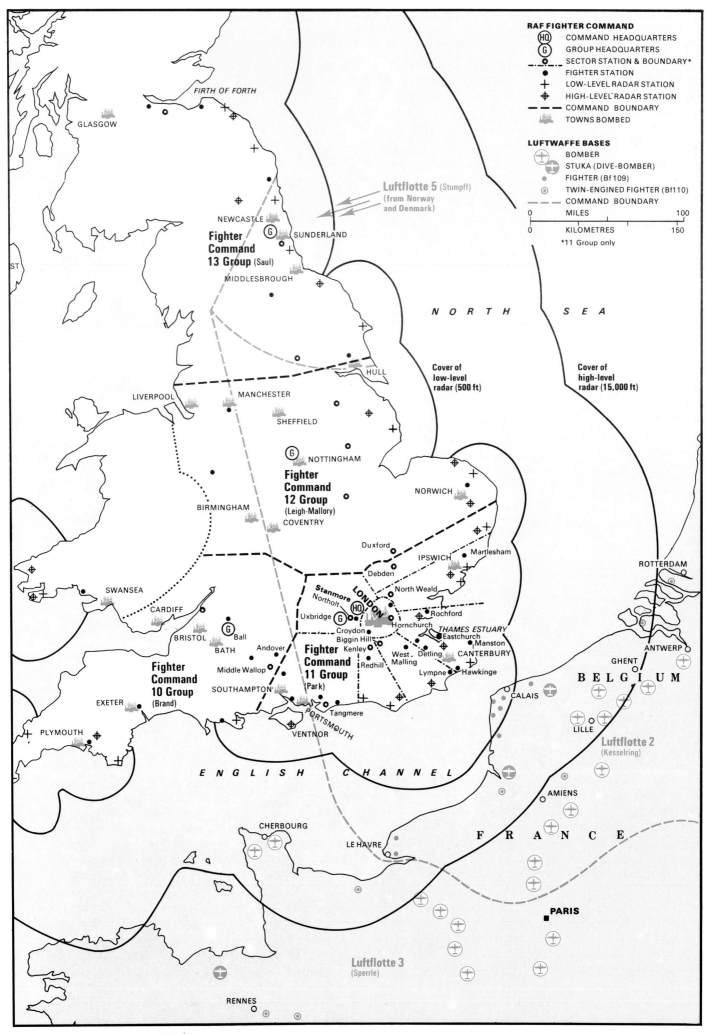

RAF FIGHTER COMMAND
- (HQ) COMMAND HEADQUARTERS
- (G) GROUP HEADQUARTERS
- SECTOR STATION & BOUNDARY*
- FIGHTER STATION
- LOW-LEVEL RADAR STATION
- HIGH-LEVEL RADAR STATION
- COMMAND BOUNDARY
- TOWNS BOMBED

LUFTWAFFE BASES
- BOMBER
- STUKA (DIVE-BOMBER)
- FIGHTER (Bf 109)
- TWIN-ENGINED FIGHTER (Bf 110)
- COMMAND BOUNDARY

MILES 0 — 100
KILOMETRES 0 — 150
*11 Group only

GLASGOW

FIRTH OF FORTH

NEWCASTLE
SUNDERLAND

Fighter Command 13 Group (Saul)

Luftflotte 5 (Stumpff) (from Norway and Denmark)

MIDDLESBROUGH

N O R T H   S E A

Cover of low-level radar (500 ft)

Cover of high-level radar (15,000 ft)

HULL

LIVERPOOL
MANCHESTER
SHEFFIELD

NOTTINGHAM

Fighter Command 12 Group (Leigh-Mallory)

BIRMINGHAM

COVENTRY

NORWICH

Duxford
IPSWICH   Martlesham
Debden

ROTTERDAM

SWANSEA
CARDIFF

Stanmore
Northolt   LONDON
Uxbridge
Croydon
Biggin Hill
Kenley

North Weald
Rochford
Hornchurch

THAMES ESTUARY
Eastchurch
Manston
CANTERBURY
West Malling   Detling
Redhill
Lympne   Hawkinge

ANTWERP

GHENT

B E L G I U M

BRISTOL
Ball
BATH
Andover
Middle Wallop
SOUTHAMPTON

Fighter Command 10 Group (Brand)

EXETER
PLYMOUTH

Fighter Command 11 Group (Park)

Tangmere
PORTSMOUTH
VENTNOR

CALAIS

LILLE

Luftflotte 2 (Kesselring)

E N G L I S H   C H A N N E L

AMIENS

CHERBOURG

LE HAVRE

F R A N C E

PARIS

Luftflotte 3 (Sperrle)

RENNES

LEFT: *A map of the battle showing the major airfields and groups of both sides, and the effective ranges of the RAF's high and low-level radar chains.*

RIGHT: *A Spitfire over the Channel. In theory, if not always in reality, the Spitfire was used to tackle the Luftwaffe's fighter escorts. The Luftwaffe's Bf 109s, although enjoying the advantage of a forward-firing 20mm cannon in the nose, were hampered by their lack of endurance over England, sometimes as little as 20 minutes.*

some hours away. The problem was solved by having a handy supply of barley sugar sweets to suck.

There was no special flying clothing in 1940, pilots simply flew in something comfortable; an old uniform, with perhaps a jumper or pullover, covered perhaps by an overall. Neither the Hurricane or Spitfire had any cockpit heating and within minutes a pilot could be at 30,000 feet where the outside temperature was a good deal colder than on the ground! Irvin jackets too, although bulky, helped keep the body warm.

Sitting in the sun was pleasant enough but the ever-present danger was often just minutes away. At dawn readiness the pilots usually nodded off to sleep right

away, they were half asleep anyway. If there had been a binge the night before, the pilot might trot over to his airplane and take a whiff of oxygen. Another method of sobering up was used by the medical officer. He would give the pilot a special mixture tasting oddly of toothpaste, which some pilots thought it was anyway. The pilots had to be prepared to give their all in the coming battle.

Death and destruction for the RAF and the Luftwaffe continued with the commencement of the third phase of the battle on 24 August. The shortage of RAF pilots had recently become critical. Support came from the Fleet Air Arm, which lent 56 pilots during the battle. A

RIGHT: *A Spitfire of No 222 Squadron prepares to taxi to a runway. This squadron, flying from Hornchurch, lost three aircraft and two pilots on 4 September.*

further 30 or so came from Bomber and Army Co-operation Commands. Some new squadrons also became available, a Polish, a Czech and a Canadian squadron helped to swell Fighter Command's ranks or fill a gap left by a unit pulled out of the front line for a rest.

On Saturday 24 August, airfields were attacked in the southeast of England. Manston was evacuated and Portsmouth was hit heavily. North Weald was attacked by 20 bombers which hit station buildings, two messes, the married quarters and stores, but otherwise did not affect the efficiency of the base.

By mid-afternoon Keith Park had all his squadrons airborne and engaged, so he requested help from Leigh-Mallory's 12 Group. Leigh-Mallory had been keen to try and form his squadrons into wings in order to bring a larger force of fighters into action at one time. This made sense but unfortunately it took time to organize once they were in the air and more often than not in the days ahead, the raiders were on their way home before the 12 Group wing could get at them. On the 24th only the Spitfires of 19 Squadron became engaged after the failure of the wing to form over Duxford. The six pilots of 19 Squadron were flying cannon-armed Spitfires which were suffering from gun-stoppages at this stage of RAF cannon development. However, Flight Lieutenant B J E Lane's guns scored:

ABOVE: *Pilots from No 19 Squadron, including Sergeant G C Unwin (fifth from left) and Squadron Leader H J Cozens (fourth from right). Unwin was destined to lead the squadron later in the battle.*

RIGHT: *An heroic portrait of Sergeant R F Hamlyn, DFM. Flying with No 610 Squadron during the summer of 1940, he claimed a dozen air victories. On 24 August, he accounted for five enemy planes in three sorties.*

RIGHT: *A trio of three-aircraft 'vics' from No 610 Squadron patrol the skies over southeast England on the lookout for Luftwaffe formations.*

BELOW: *Two Bf 110s of ZG76, readily identifiable by the distinctive shark-tooth motif, fly over the English coast.*

'I climbed up and at approximately 1610 hours got astern of a ragged formation of about 40 Bf 110s and Do 215s, escorted by ten Bf 109s above and to the rear. I approached from below . . . and almost got within range when 110s saw us and turned towards us. A dog-fight ensued and I opened fire from below and astern of nearest 110 but was forced to break away as tracer appeared over my head from enemy aircraft astern. Got below another 110 and fired slight deflection burst at port engine and observed a large part of engine or mainplane fly off. Enemy aircraft dived and I observed it crash into the sea.'

Another pilot, Sergeant R F Hamlyn of 610 Squadron claimed the destruction of five German aircraft during the day, in three hectic sorties. Altogether the RAF flew

936 sorties on the 24th, and lost 22 aircraft. The Luftwaffe losses totaled 38 during 1030 sorties.

The following day *Luftflotte* 3 sent a large force toward Weymouth. Nos 17, 87 and 609 Squadrons engaged this raid, destroying several raiders. Flying Officer Count M B Czernin of 17 Squadron shot down two and shared a third with 609 Squadron despite seeing his commanding officer shot down ahead of him during a battle with a gaggle of Bf 110s:

'One broke. Chased and fired from above. Nose went down, EA burst into flames and crashed straight into the sea. Climbed and resumed attack. Beam attack and 110 broke

LEFT: *Pilots of No 54 Squadron relax between sorties. Standing, from left to right: Flying Officer C Gray, Pilot Officer R Blake and Pilot Officer G Gribble; seated, from left to right: Squadron Leader J Leathart, Flight Lieutenant A W A Bayne and Flight Lieutenant M Pearson.*

BELOW LEFT: *A formation of He 111s under attack as seen through the camera of an RAF fighter.*

BELOW: *Flight Sergeant D A Kingaby, a veteran of the Battle of Britain.*

and plowed along the airfield on its back. Sergeant J Davis was blown across two fields and into a river while Pilot Officer E F Edsall was blown up but landed right side up. He scrambled clear to help Deere out of his smashed airplane as bombs continued to rain down. All three pilots were ready for action the next day.

As August ended it became evident to Luftwaffe commanders that despite the claims of its fighter pilots, the RAF was far from being knocked out of the sky. They also realized that the output of fighter production from British factories and from repair depots had been considerably underestimated. The German bomber crews continued to report aggressive actions by RAF fighters. There was not the slightest sign that the British boys were relaxing in their determination to get to grips with the enemy.

Despite this view, Fighter Command's reserves were running dangerously low but it could just maintain sup-

port for 10, 11 and 12 Group's losses. Dowding's main concern was for pilots, especially leaders. A dozen squadron commanders had been killed or wounded and nearly 40 flight commanders had similarly been knocked out. On some sorties, sections, flights and, on occasion, even whole squadrons were led by junior officers and experienced non-commissioned officer pilots, such as Ginger Lacey (501 Squadron), Geoffrey Allard (85), Archie McDowell (602) and 'Grumpy' Unwin (19). Of all the experienced fighter pilots in Dowding's force, there were only about 500 officers or sergeants and each had to fly four, five or even six sorties each day.

It was inevitable that replacement pilots from training units had not the length of training that would have been desirable. Some became easy prey to a still victorious Luftwaffe fighter arm. The squadrons were taking a battering. No 151 Squadron was pulled back

RIGHT: *Pilots of No 610 Squadron wait for the order to scramble, Kenley, August 1940.*

BELOW: *Flight Lieutenant Geoffrey 'Sammy' Allard, DFC, DFM, of No 85 Squadron fought in France and throughout the Battle of Britain, claiming two dozen victories. He was killed in a flying accident in 1941.*

BELOW RIGHT: *RAF groundcrew prepare a fighter for its next sortie.*

from the front, down to 10 aircraft and 12 pilots. No 56, without a commanding officer and with only seven aircraft went to a quieter location. No 43 had lost two commanding officers and its third, Squadron Leader C B Hull, was to last just one week. No 610 Squadron was about to leave for the north and a rest. The fate of Britain now rested totally on the young shoulders of Fighter Command's pilots as September began.

The first day of September saw the continuance of attacks on air bases with four major assaults. Biggin Hill was attacked for the sixth time in three days. No 79 Squadron was now Biggin's only defense and pilots returning from an interception found the airfield pitted with bomb craters, forcing them to divert to Croydon. Eastchurch, Detling and the docks at Tilbury were other targets. Over 120 raiders returned to these targets after lunch while two further raids went for Hawkinge, Lympne and Detling in the late afternoon. In the

last raid Biggin was hit yet again, knocking out the operations room. Four Spitfires were also destroyed and the armory set ablaze.

On 2 September, there were four raids. This time Eastchurch, North Weald, Rochford and again Biggin Hill were attacked. The raiders totaled around 250 aircraft, an awe-inspiring sight for individual squadrons to see flying in.

Two tragic losses occurred on the 1st and 2nd. Two fighter-pilot brothers fell within hours of each other. On 1 September Flying Officer Patrick Woods-Scawen of 85 Squadron died when leading his section. No 85 Squadron was led by Flight Sergeant Allard against a vast armada of aircraft, but enemy fighters hurled themselves at the squadron to shoot down five of the Hurricanes. One pilot was killed, two wounded and one missing (the fifth crash-landed unhurt). The missing pilot was Woods-Scawen who was found on the 6th – his

parachute had failed to open. The next day his brother Tony, flying with 43 Squadron, was shot down by Bf 109s just 24 hours after his brother. Both had won the DFC in the battle.

Also on the 2nd, Pilot Officer R H Hillary of 603 Squadron shot down two Bf 109s, probably a third and damaged a fourth in three sorties. On the second sortie, just after midday:

'When five miles off Sheppey I saw a formation of 109s. I chased one over to France and fired at it. I saw the EA's perspex hood break up but as it was a head-on attack I was unable to see anything more of it. I then saw a squadron of 109s at the same height as myself, 23,000 feet . . . I attacked outside Bf 109 with three short bursts and saw it spin down emitting black and white smoke. After a few seconds it caught fire.'

Sergeant J H Ginger Lacey, flying in 501 Squadron, also destroyed a Bf 109. He saw three Messerschmitts about to dive on his squadron and climbed to engage them:

'I was able to get in a good burst of about five seconds at a red cowled Bf 109, but the EA immediately turned and I was unable to bring my guns to bear, but after about 30 seconds of circling, the Bf 109 pilot jumped out and did a delayed drop of about 5,000 feet before opening his parachute.'

The next day, the first anniversary of the war, more heavy attacks were directed against the southern airfields, the now familiar build up of aircraft over Calais coming on to the radar screens around 0800 hours. Their allotted targets were Hornchurch, North Weald and Debden, although North Weald was the only one reached by the raiders. One of the defending fighter pilots was the same Richard Hillary of 603 Squadron who had done so well the day before. He later wrote of his feelings as he sat in his Spitfire following the scramble call:

'I felt the usual sick feeling in the pit of my stomach, as though I was about to run a race, and then I was too busy getting into position to feel anything.'

Making the mistake of following a 109 for too long he was himself attacked from behind. His Spitfire burst into flames and for several agonizing seconds he was trapped in the blazing cockpit before the machine broke up and he was flung into space. He, like Tom Gleave, was very badly burned and spent months in hospital. Later he wrote his classic book *The Last Enemy*.

Sergeant D Fopp of 17 Squadron was also shot down and burned on the 3rd:

'We were scrambled late and did not get sufficient altitude to achieve a favourable attacking position from above, with the result that we had to attack head-on at about 20,000 feet, and hope to break up the large formation of Do 17s, with guns blazing which did separate them considerably. I had just put a Dornier's engine out and he was smoking badly when I saw three Bf 110s coming in behind in line astern. By this time I had run out of ammunition but decided that as I could not match them for speed I would turn into them and simulate an attack. This I did and to my astonishment and joy they broke all round me so I immediately half rolled and dived for the deck. Unfortunately for me one of them was also below and behind out of sight and managed to put a cannon shell into my radiator, with the result that all I heard was a thump and the next second I was sitting in a ball of fire.'

Fopp managed to bale out and put out his smoldering tunic and trousers. He landed in trees but got out of his harness safely, walked out of the wood and met two farm laborers. In his condition he could have been any nationality but his language was such that they were quickly convinced that he was British!

Pilot Officer D W Hanson, also of 17 Squadron, shot down a Dornier in this action but his machine was hit by return fire. Hanson had difficulty in getting out of his Hurricane and when finally he succeeded he was only 100 feet up. His parachute failed to deploy in the short drop and he was killed when he hit the ground almost at the same moment as his machine crashed on Foulness Island.

Honors were even on the war's first anniversary – 16 Germans shot down, for 16 RAF fighters and eight pilots.

It was slightly better the next day, 25 Germans for 17 RAF machines. The Germans went for sector RAF stations and the Vickers factory at Brooklands. A force of Bf 110s got through the defenses by flying at low level

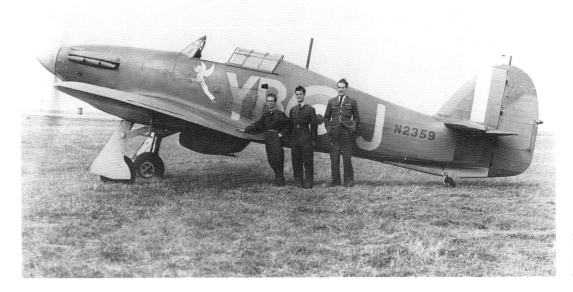

LEFT: *Pilot Officer Stevens poses with LACs McEvoy and Jaquest beside his Hurricane from No 17 Squadron, Debden.*

RIGHT: *The remains of a Bf 109E of JG53 'Udet' flown by Franz von Werra, the only German to escape from a British prisoner of war camp. He was the victim of a No 234 Squadron Spitfire on the afternoon of 5 September.*

BELOW: *Rearming a Spitfire Mark 1a of No 19 Squadron at Duxford, September 1940.*

BELOW RIGHT: *Flight Lieutenant W Rhodes-Moorhouse, son of a World War I VC winner, claimed nine victories before his death in combat on 6 September.*

and following the railroad track over Guildford. They hit Brooklands, where Wellington bombers were being built. Alert ground gunners shot down two Bf 110s and others hurriedly got rid of their bombs, as Hurricanes of 253 Squadron got in among them, but nevertheless the Germans did considerable damage. Some 88 workers were killed and 600 were injured. Output almost stopped for four days as machine and erecting shops were badly damaged. Several Bf 110s were shot down by the Hurricanes.

No 253 Squadron was based at Kenley, sharing the field with 66 Squadron who did not have a good day. They lost five of their Spitfires and all the pilots involved were wounded. No 222 Squadron from Hornchurch lost three Spitfires and two pilots were killed. As if enemy fighters were not dangerous enough, Pilot Officer J M V Carpenter was hit by 'friendly' anti-aircraft fire over Kent and blown out of his cockpit. He landed in his parachute with only slight injuries. The next day 66 Squadron lost three more aircraft, while 41

Squadron lost five including the squadron commander and one flight commander. No 19 Squadron also lost its commanding officer on the 5th.

On Friday 6 September, the final day of phase three, it was the Polish pilots of 303 Squadron who suffered at the hands of the Luftwaffe. Five of their aircraft were shot down although no pilots were killed. The squadron's joint commanding officers, Squadron Leader R G Kellett an Englishman, and Squadron Leader Z Krasnodebski, were both wounded. Both British flight commanders were also shot down and a Polish noncommissioned officer was wounded.

Four pilots from 601 Squadron based at Tangmere were shot down, two of whom were killed. One was Flying Officer C R Davis, an experienced South African pilot with several victories to his name, the other was Flying Officer Willie Rhodes-Moorhouse.

The Luftwaffe lost 378 of its aircraft during the third phase. The margin between victory and defeat was now very slender.

THE BLITZ

The battle's fourth phase, marked by a change of tactics by the Luftwaffe, began on 7 September. It was clear now to the Luftwaffe High Command that RAF resistance was far from decreasing. During the period 24 August to 6 September, over 100 bombers had been lost despite the orders to German fighter pilots to stick close and defend the bomber formations. It appeared also that despite continual raids on RAF airfields, they were not being knocked out for any appreciable length of time.

Some believed that London should be the direct target, thereby causing the civilian population to crack and force the British Government to capitulate. Bombs had in fact been dropped on London by navigational error on the night of 25 August, which caused the reprisal raid already mentioned. Hitler gave Goering a free hand and it was just as well for Britain that he did, for Goering ended his attacks on RAF airfields in order to concentrate on the plum of a prize – London. It was to prove an incalculable error, but it saved Fighter Command. Plans were immediately put into operation to fly against London and the first assault took place on the 7th.

Prepared for further attacks on its airfields, the RAF was not even considering a raid on London when the radar screens showed a massive armada of aircraft heading toward the Thames Estuary – 300 bombers escorted by 600 fighters in two waves. The first wave flew direct to the estuary, the other passed over central London before turning back to the estuary and the East End of London. Caught on the hop, the defending RAF fighters were unable to engage before many of the German aircraft had dropped their bombs. So while the airfields were being adequately defended, the road to London was open. Finally 11 Group got some units to intercept the huge armada and thereafter Hurricanes and Spitfires tried to nibble at them all the way back to the coast. It was to cost both sides dearly.

No 12 Group's Big Wing got into action, with 19, 242 and 310 Squadrons making preparations, when anti-aircraft fire attracted them to part of the raid near

North Weald. Squadron Leader B J E Lane, now commanding officer of 19 Squadron, saw them and attacked the enemy aircraft:

'A 110 dived in front of me and I led A Flight after it. Two Hurricanes were also attacking it. I fired a short burst as well as the other aircraft. Two baled out, one parachute failing to open. Enemy aircraft crashed one mile east of Hornchurch and one crewman landed nearby and was taken prisoner of war.'

Flight Lieutenant J H G McArthur of 609 Squadron went for a formation of bombers which he took to be

PREVIOUS PAGES: *One of the most famous images of the Blitz on London – the dome of St Paul's shrouded in dense smoke following a Luftwaffe raid.*

ABOVE: *A pair of Dornier Do 17s of Kampfgeschwader 3 over Canning Town on 7 September 1940, the first day of the Blitz.*

LEFT: *The aftermath of the 7 September raid which caused severe damage in London's docklands.*

RIGHT: *Thick, acrid smoke billows from burning oil tanks after a Luftwaffe raid.*

BELOW: *Do 17s of KG3 cross the River Thames heading for the East End.*

Dorniers (Dornier 17s and Bf 110s were often confused during the battle):

'I went for the nearest bomber and opened fire at about 400 yards, meanwhile experiencing very heavy return cross fire from the bomber formation. After about 12 seconds smoke started to come from the port motor and it left the formation . . . I waited until it got down to about 3000 feet and then

dived vertically on to it and fired off the rest of my ammunition. It kept going on down seemingly still under some sort of control, until it hit the water about 10 miles out from the centre of the Thames Estuary.'

Casualties among the RAF defenders totaled 28 fighters and 19 pilots. Some were experienced pilots and leaders. No 43 Squadron lost Caesar Hull, who had won his DFC in the Norwegian campaign earlier in the year, and Flight Lieutenant R C Reynell, the Hawker test pilot who was flying operationally with the squadron. No 234 Squadron lost its commanding officer, Joe O'Brien, as well as its senior flight commander, Flight Lieutenant P C Hughes, DFC, who had claimed 16 victories in two months. Hughes was attacking a Dornier when its wing ripped off and smashed into his Spitfire, causing him to crash. No 257 Squadron was bounced by Bf 109s and lost four aircraft and two pilots, including Flight Lieutenant H R A Beresford. It was not until 1979 that his remains and his shattered Hurricane were found in marshy ground on the Isle of Sheppey. No 303 Polish Squadron lost two aircraft with two more damaged. One of the damaged aircraft was flown by the British Flight Lieutenant A S Forbes who was slightly wounded. No 249 Squadron from North Weald lost six Hurricanes and one pilot plus three more wounded in fights with Bf 109s.

German casualties totaled 41, of which 15 were Bf 109s and seven were 110s. London had been heavily bombed and nearly 450 people had been killed in both central and suburban areas with over 1300 injured. The new phase in the Luftwaffe's offensive against Britain had begun. London and its populace would now have to 'take it' but at least the pressure was taken off Dowding's sorely pressed fighter bases. In addition the Luftwaffe began flying against London by night.

The next day the air action was light by recent standards and only night raids affected London, but on the 9th the battle flared again. London was bombed and raids were directed against factories in the Thames Estuary area as well as Brooklands. Some 28 German aircraft were shot down as against 19 British machines. Two days later, on 11 September, the losses were 25 German aircraft and a depressing 29 RAF aircraft with 17 pilots killed and six others wounded, during raids on London, Portsmouth and Southampton.

Keith Park was now, whenever possible, ordering paired squadrons to be used together. When squadrons at 'readiness' were sent against early raiders, the Spitfires would take on the escort fighters while an accompanying Hurricane unit went for the bombers. In their turn, the 'available' – 15 minutes – squadrons, brought to the 'readiness' state were in pairs, to be ready to deal with subsequent waves of raiders. The 'available' –

LEFT: *A Heinkel He 111 bomber flies over the Silvertown district of London.*

RIGHT: *The devastating effect of a bomb blast in a London street, 8/9 September; rescue workers comb the rubble for survivors.*

BELOW: *The daytime sky over the Palace of Westminster, crisscrossed by vapor trails as Luftwaffe and RAF aircraft clash.*

at 30 minutes – squadrons were then used singly to reinforce those units already engaged or to protect specific factory or airfield targets.

On the 11th, big enemy formations began to build up over Calais and Ostend in the early afternoon while others began to fly in from the Seine area and Cher-

bourg. Shortly afterward waves of Bf 109s were in evidence over Kent. It was these Bf 109s, as well as close escort 109s, that caused many of the RAF casualties.

Only two RAF pilots were lost on 12 September, but one was Wing Commander J S Dewar DSO, DFC, wing commander at Exeter and late commanding officer of 87 Squadron. He had been visiting friends at Tangmere and took off with them during an alert. He failed to return and later his bullet-ridden body was found where he had fallen in his parachute. A few days later one of his old 87 Squadron's pilots chased a bomber 20 miles out to sea to shoot it down in personal revenge for Dewar's death.

The issue of shooting up pilots in their parachutes is a controversial one, but it did happen from time to time on both sides. One former Battle of Britain pilot told this author that in his squadron they had an unwritten law that if a German pilot was in his parachute over the French coast or within 10 miles of it they might have a go at him, but not if he was coming down over England or off the English coast. One of his companions was always for shooting them up wherever he found them!

The 13 September was also quiet, although one of the RAF's successful non-commissioned officer pilots, Ginger Lacey, had to take to his parachute after engaging a He 111 over Kent. It was a cloudy day and Lacey had volunteered to go up to try to locate a reported raider. Guided by ground control he found his prey and shot it down but his Hurricane was hit by return fire and he had to bale out. Later he was told that this Heinkel had bombed Buckingham Palace.

London was again attacked on the 14th although poor weather prevented any large-scale assault until the afternoon. A little after 1500 hours three groups of raiders crossed the English coast and headed in along two routes – the Estuary and over Kent. Most of the raiders were fighters and in the scraps which occurred honors proved even, 14 to each side.

SGT. J.H.LACEY. D.F.M.

Yet it was to be the next day which turned out to be significant in many respects. For ever afterward, 15 September every year has been set aside as the Anniversary Day of the Battle of Britain. It saw the Germans heavily defeated in the air and ultimately the Germans were forced to change their policy against Britain.

ABOVE: *Sergeant J H 'Ginger' Lacey of No 501 Squadron was one of the top-scoring pilots of the battle and was responsible for downing the Heinkel He 111 which bombed Buckingham Palace on 13 September. Hit by return fire during the attack, Lacey had to take to his parachute.*

LEFT: *Purfleet under attack, 7 September 1940.*

For the Germans it was a repeat of the 7 September raid, in that it was supposed to be a prelude to invasion. Hitler had postponed his planned assault by sea and air, from early September to the 11th. Then he postponed it again to the 17th. However, the disastrous results of the 15th caused him to postpone the invasion indefinitely.

While it is felt in some quarters that Hitler never seriously considered invading Britain, there is no doubt that the people of Britain, and especially the war leaders, could see no other course open to Hitler.

By 1100 hours on Sunday 15 September mass formations of German aircraft clearly showed on the radar

ABOVE: *Londoners taking shelter in Aldwych underground station. Although officially frowned upon, sleeping below ground during Luftwaffe air raids became a common practice.*

ABOVE RIGHT: *The smoking ruins of a London street after a raid.*

RIGHT: *One of the less practical designs for a bomb shelter.*

screens. Even at this stage the Germans had not totally realized how accurately the radar plots could identify the size, course and height of their raids. No 11 Group scrambled 11 squadrons, 10 Group one and 12 Group its Big Wing of five squadrons.

As the Germans flew in from the coast toward London, in layers from 15,000-26,000 feet, they were continually harassed by RAF fighters whose young pilots flung themselves relentlessly at the vast horde of black-crossed bombers and fighters.

The tenacity of the RAF fighter pilots, as well as the sheer number of fighters they could see, must have come as a great shock to many Luftwaffe fliers. It had been confidently predicted that Fighter Command was down to its last 'handful' of aircraft, and yet the Luft-

waffe could see flight after flight, squadron after squadron, heading straight for them, their wing guns blazing. One of the attackers was Flying Officer J C Dundas of 609 Squadron:

'(We) turned towards enemy aircraft which we identified as Dorniers and turned to intercept. There were many 109s on both sides of the bombers and above them . . . I turned and attacked the EA in centre of formation from below and from the beam. As I passed I saw one of its motors stop. On breaking away I was attacked by a 109 from above and astern . . . I was chased off by three 109s which peeled off from 20,000 feet above, but who gave themselves away by opening fire from excessive range.'

Squadron Leader J Sample, commanding officer of 504 Squadron also got in among the Dorniers. He attacked

RIGHT: *The remains of a row of terraced houses after a direct hit. Despite the severity of the raids, the morale of London's civilian population remained remarkably high for the most part.*

BELOW: *Firefighters dowse the remains of Hauptmann Ernst Püttman's KG3 Dornier Do 17Z-2 after it had crashed into the forecourt of Victoria station on 15 September.*

one which broke formation streaming smoke. Looking down he clearly saw the famous bend in the River Thames and also picked out the Oval cricket ground:

'I found myself below another Dornier which had white smoke coming from it. It was being attacked by two Hurricanes and a Spitfire . . . I went to join in. I climbed up above and did a diving attack on him. Coming in to attack I noticed what appeared to be a red light shining in the rear gunner's cockpit but when I got closer I realised I was looking right through the gunner's cockpit into the pilot and observer's cockpit beyond. The red light was fire. I gave it a quick burst and as I passed him on the right I looked through the big glass nose of the Dornier. It was like a furnace inside. He began to go down and we watched. In a few seconds the tail came off and the bomber did a forward somersault and then went into a spin. After he had done two turns in his spin his wings broke off outboard of the engines.'

Sergeant R T Holmes of Sample's squadron gained undying fame by shooting down a Dornier which crashed into the forecourt of Victoria Station. Holmes was hit by return fire and baled out, only to land ingloriously in a Chelsea garbage can.

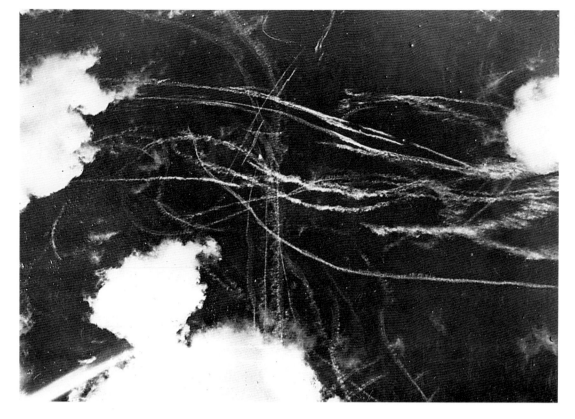

LEFT: *Vapor trails over Kent, 18 September.*

As the assault continued into the afternoon, other units took to the air. One pilot airborne was the station commander of RAF Northolt, a fighter pilot from World War I, Group Captain S F Vincent. He was near Biggin Hill when he saw 18 Dorniers escorted by 20 Bf 109s:

'There was no other British fighters in sight, so I made a head-on attack on the first section of the bombers, opening fire at 600 yards and closing to 200 yards. I saw my DeWilde ammunition hit the EA. On breaking away I noticed that five of the bombers had turned round and were proceeding due south. I made further attacks on the retreating bombers . . .

and could see the DeWilde hitting in each attack. One Dornier left the formation and lost height. With no ammunition left I could not finish it off.'

John Dundas was back in the air for another crack and again found Dornier bombers, this time above Rye:

'Red section attacked the rear wing of Dorniers and as they did so two Dorniers detached themselves from formation and tried to dive away. I selected one and went in after it had been attacked by a number of Red Section. Fired from 300 to 150 yards and closed to dead astern and slightly above. At first I

LEFT: *An antiaircraft battery in action at night. Although the guns had great difficulty in hitting enemy aircraft, their fire often forced Luftwaffe pilots to make evasive maneuvers.*

RIGHT: *Flight Lieutenant Stan Turner, DFC, fought with No 242 Squadron and was credited with 10 kills in engagements over France and England.*

RIGHT: *Flight Lieutenant Stan Turner, DFC, fought with No 242 Squadron and was credited with 10 kills in engagements over France and England.*

experienced return fire and was twice hit. Then pieces began to fall off and flames came from its starboard wing and engine. After breaking away I saw EA spin down and members of the crew escape by parachute.'

Pilot Officer P S Turner, flying with 242 Squadron in 12 Group's Wing, was in the action, sending down a Bf 109 probably destroyed before he attacked a Dornier:

'. . . observed a Do 215, attacked from abeam using full deflection. His starboard engine started to smoke, the 215 then slid into a gentle dive. It hit the ground and exploded between some houses on the north bank of the Thames east of Hornchurch. No people left the aircraft.'

Yet again German Intelligence estimates were wrong. The RAF's 'last 50 Spitfires' was only a figure on their reports. Although at the time an inflated figure of 185 German aircraft shot down put great heart into the British people and the RAF pilots, the true figure was 60. Even so, with damaged machines taken into account it was a savage blow to the Luftwaffe, particularly in view of recent air losses. The RAF lost 26 fighters.

RIGHT: *Firefighters play their hoses onto fiercely burning buildings in an attempt to prevent them from collapsing.*

5
THE
TURNING
POINT

Although the battle was to rage for several more weeks and the RAF fighter pilots had to continue their constant air actions against the Luftwaffe, it has now become accepted that 15 September was the turning point. As if to accentuate the victory of the 15th, the skies over southern England stayed comparatively quiet on the 16th.

Goering called a conference with his air commanders. Although presumably shaken by the losses of the previous day he showed little sign of it and merely informed his commanders that there was to be a return to a policy of knocking out the RAF – a task he felt would now only take four or five days. In this he was supported by his intelligence people who still continued to underestimate both the RAF's front-line strength and reserves. These reserves now numbered 160 with a further 400 available for delivery in seven days.

Goering also decided to reduce the bomber formations but to support them with maximum fighter cover in order to blast the British fighters as they came up to engage the raids. London would continue to be raided by night.

The 11 Group commander, Keith Park, was also adjusting his tactics. He felt that his squadrons could do better if more were able to engage the enemy. Specifically, he wanted the Spitfires from Biggin Hill and Hornchurch to engage the Bf 109s, while Hurricanes, operating in groups of three if time allowed them to get together, from Northolt and Tangmere, went for the bombers. It also became clear that the claim of 185 kills on the 15th was not supported by crashed aircraft on the ground, and the figure was being revised.

Activity was still reduced on the 18th although it was obvious to the RAF that a large fighter sweep flown by the Luftwaffe in the afternoon was designed solely in order to produce a fighter-versus-fighter action. In an attempt to carry out Goering's directives, the Luftwaffe mounted another sweep the following morning, fol-

lowed by a small raiding force of Ju 88s escorted by 100 Messerschmitts. This was ignored by the RAF as its intention was too obvious. Therefore, another force of Ju 88s was sent in. This was met by a large number of Hurricanes and Spitfires, including the 12 Group Duxford Wing. Nine Ju 88s were quickly destroyed by 92 Squadron and the Big Wing, although the Wing claimed 30 victories!

The most significant event on the 19th was that Hitler finally shelved his plans to invade England and ordered the prepared invasion fleet of barges and troops to be dispersed. This latter fact was confirmed by RAF

PAGE 64: *RAF personnel remove the wreckage of a Bf 109E of JG27 which crash-landed in Windsor Great Park after combat with Spitfires on 30 September.*

ABOVE: *A Dornier Do 17Z bomber heads for southeast England. Although combat proven, this type, like all of the Luftwaffe's bomber forces, had a short range when fully laden and was vulnerable to fighter attack during daylight raids.*

LEFT: *An air-to-air view of a Dornier formation.*

reconnaissance which, naturally, had been taking a keen interest in watching this force grow in recent weeks in the Channel ports along the French coast.

Over the next few days Luftwaffe activity was slight, confined mostly to fighter sweeps. Then on the 27th the fury returned. At 0800 hours activity was recorded on Operations Tables – bomb-carrying Bf 109s and Bf 110s headed in toward London on a broad front from Dover to Brighton. The 11 Group fighters harried them all the way to the outskirts of London. The Germans remained over the southeast, trying to exhaust the defender's fuel and ammunition supplies preparatory to a raid by Ju

88s. However, the bombers failed to pick up their heavy escort and met over 100 defending fighters which promptly set about the raiders. Urgent calls for supporting Bf 109s brought in a large force of Messerschmitts and both raiders and defenders suffered losses. Twelve Ju 88s went crashing earthward in this battle. One of the defending Bf 109s was shot down by Pilot Officer R G A Barclay of 249 Squadron:

'I chased a 109 which dived very steeply. I had to use automatic boost cut-out to catch up the 109. I lost the 109 in haze owing to its camouflage against the ground, but it suddenly

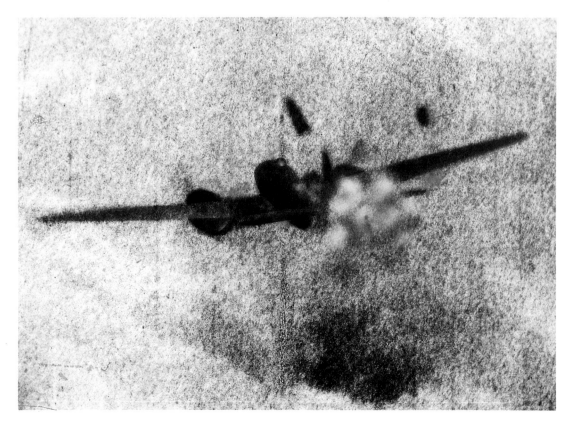

LEFT: *Pilot Officer G Davis of No 222 Squadron. He shot down a He 111 on 30 August but was himself shot down and wounded on the next day. He went on to win a DFC in Burma during 1944.*

climbed almost vertically out of the haze. I closed to about 150 yards and fired about four bursts, one almost vertically up at the 109, one almost vertically down at the 109, two bursts from the beam. The EA poured glycol. The cockpit roof flew off. The pilot baled out successfully. The EA crashed on a farm SW of Ashford.'

Later, on the squadron's third sortie of the day, Barclay destroyed a Ju 88 but had to force land at West Malling when his Hurricane was hit by a Bf 109's snap burst. Pilot Officer A G Lewis of 249 claimed six victories on this day, three Bf 109s, two Bf 110s and a Ju 88. He also damaged another Bf 109 and probably destroyed a Bf 110. It brought his personal score to 18.

Farther west 80 aircraft were heading for Bristol; He 111s and bomb-carrying Bf 110s escorted by more Bf 110s, came over the coast. This raid was met by five RAF squadrons. The Heinkels were split up and sent scurrying for the coast, the Bf 110s pressed on to Bristol but were hotly engaged by RAF fighters. One escorting Bf 110 was shot down by Pilot Officer M C Maxwell of 56 Squadron. Having scrambled, Maxwell had to land, but taking off afterward he attacked alone:

'At 16,000 feet saw a formation of about 25 EA ahead at 18,000 feet, climbed and made a stern attack on rear aircraft. I then broke away and saw EA losing height with black smoke emitting from port engine. Another Hurricane attacked EA which dived steeply and later I attacked again after Hurricane broke away, and saw EA with one engine stopped, crash after endeavouring to force land.'

Total losses by the Luftwaffe numbered 55 including 21 bombers; the RAF lost 28 fighters. At the time the day

LEFT: *King George VI in conversation with Air Vice-Marshal Keith Park during a visit to RAF Northolt, 26 September 1940. The station commander, Stanley Vincent, is second from left.*

RIGHT: *Flight Lieutenant R Lee, DSO, DFC, and Flying Officer A Lewis, DFC, pilots of No 85 Squadron. Lee was shot down and killed on 18 August.*

ranked with 15 August and 15 September as a victory against the German Air Force.

In contrast the 28th saw a victory for the Luftwaffe fighters, for during attacks on London and the Solent they shot down 16 RAF aircraft and only lost two of their own in actual combat. One of the RAF men shot down was A G Lewis who had scored so heavily the previous day. Bf 109s hit him over Faversham – he baled out with burns.

The final fury of September came on the last day of the month when Bf 109s flew sweeps toward London in the morning. No 229 Squadron suffered badly, losing four Hurricanes and four damaged in fights with Bf 109s, with one pilot killed and three others wounded. This raid was followed by Bf 109s and Bf 110s attacking the Weymouth area and then after lunch Ju 88s and Bf 109s again made for London. The final raid consisted of He 111s and Bf 110s going for the Westland factory at Yeovil. No 56 Squadron was attacked by Bf 110s, losing five Hurricanes with two others damaged, but luckily no pilots were lost. No 152 Squadron also tangled with the Bf 110s, losing one pilot and aircraft and damaging four Spitfires. However, overall the Germans lost 47 aircraft during the day, to the RAF's 20. Most of the Luftwaffe's casualties were Bf 109s.

We now realize that by the end of September the battle had effectively been won in the air. The German Luftwaffe could no longer sustain the losses which Fighter Command had inflicted upon it and tactics were again changed. The battle was continued by the Germans but now fighters generally flew alone. It became known as 'Messerschmitt Month.'

RIGHT: *A No 32 Squadron Hurricane taxies out from dispersal at the forward landing strip at RAF Hawkinge, Kent.*

6
FIGHTER
COMMAND
TRIUMPHS

The October battles were in many ways more dangerous than the hectic days of the previous weeks. The Bf 109s flew high, often above 25,000 feet, and the RAF fighters had to climb hard through hazy autumn sunshine and cloud to reach them. The advantage was usually held by the Bf 109s above. During these weeks the RAF lost many veteran fighters in this moment of victory.

For the defenders it was impossible to know which of the Messerschmitts carried bombs and which did not. Also, once those carrying bombs had dropped them they became again a dangerous adversary.

One veteran pilot shot down and wounded on the very first day of October was Pilot Officer G H Bennions of 41 Squadron. Having already shot down 11 German aircraft plus five probables, he was due for leave but wanted to bring his score to a neat dozen. Flying high on patrol he became separated from his companions when he went after a bunch of Bf 109s, one of which he destroyed. His machine was then hit and a cannon shell exploded by the left side of his face. His left eye was destroyed and a hole in his skull exposed his brain. In addition he sustained wounds to his right arm and leg. He managed to bale out and it was pure willpower that ultimately pulled him through.

Skirmishes occurred during the first week of October in poor weather. This improved on Monday the 7th, and the Luftwaffe sent an almost continuous stream of Bf 109s over southeast England and later a Ju 88 raid was made against the Westland plant at Yeovil. Among the RAF scorers was the 'boss' of 609 Squadron, who had

taken command of the squadron two days previously, Squadron Leader M L Robinson:

'It was extremely bright and as we were heading into the sun it was very difficult to pick out the EA which were now ahead of . . . saw a circle of 110s directly ahead of us and proceeded to attack. I broke away downwards without seeing the result of the attack and I climbed up and attacked a separate 110 from astern. A Hurricane carried out a deflection shot between 110 and myself but I went on firing when the Hurricane broke away and the 110 dived vertically down with its port motor smoking.'

Minutes later he shot down a second 110 which dived into the ground north of the coastline. The day ended with 21 German and 17 RAF aircraft lost.

The RAF was now flying patrol lines in order to be in the air and ready to engage hostile raids. When the raids came in, other squadrons took off to be covered by those already airborne. Once the new squadron was at a good height, then the covering squadron could be sent to engage raiders or land to refuel as necessary. However, with Bf 109s flying as high as 32,000 feet, it was a dangerous game, the Bf 109s always holding the advantage of height. It took the average Spitfire Mk 1 18 minutes to climb to 25,000 feet, and 21 minutes for a Hurricane.

On 8 October the RAF lost only four aircraft but managed to shoot down 14 Germans. One of the Allied pilots lost was Sergeant Joseph Frantisek, a Czech pilot flying with 303 Polish Squadron. He had already destroyed 17 Luftwaffe aircraft during September, and was the high-

RIGHT: *Squadron Leader Bob Stanford Tuck, DSO, DFC, commanded No 257 Squadron during the Battle of Britain and was one of the RAF's top pilots during World War II.*

est scoring pilot of the battle. He had shot down 11 Germans in Poland and France – making 28 in total. He was killed in a crash at RAF Northolt. Another high-scoring pilot was shot down on the 10th, Pilot Officer R F T Doe of 238 Squadron. He baled out wounded near Poole. He had 15 victories.

Over the next few days Bf 109s continued to try, and often succeeded, in penetrating to London where they dropped their bombs in random fashion. RAF fighters continued to climb up and engage these raiders but often combat claims of both sides were more or less even. However, night raids were on the increase. The

PAGE 70: *A scene common on both sides of the Channel during the Battle of Britain. In this case it is Luftwaffe personnel who wait for their orders rather than their RAF counterparts.*

LEFT: *A Czechoslovakian pilot climbs from his Hurricane with mascot in tow. Eighty-five Czech pilots fought for the RAF in the battle; eight were killed in action.*

RIGHT: *Three WAAFs decorated with the Military Medal for their part in the battle. From left to right: Sergeant J Mortimer, Corporal E Henderson and Sergeant E Turner.*

RAF had won the day battle but it was weak in night defense. Despite Britain's preoccupation with building a night-bomber force to use against Germany, it had badly neglected a night-defense plan. Antiaircraft fire was really the first line of defense. Apart from this the RAF struggled along with Blenheims, Defiants, Spitfires and Hurricanes, but the latter, despite some successes, were not designed for this role. One day fighter pilot described a night sortie as trying to locate a fly in the Albert Hall, in the dark, without airborne radar!

The day fighting continued throughout the month, Spitfires and Hurricanes and Messerschmitts tangling in the autumn sky. Pilot Officer Weir wrote:

'We generally get told to patrol at 15,000 feet below the Huns, who dive from the south straight out of the sun. Also, whatever we are told, we climb as high as we can, preferably inland first and then out to meet what is obviously fighters, though one has to go and make sure they are not bombers. I see no point in engaging 109s at 30,000 feet as they can do no harm up there.'

The 29 October brought the last big clash, with raids upon London and Southampton. No 602 Squadron, having managed to gain a tactical advantage of height and position, found themselves above the Bf 109s for a change. In company with 222 Squadron they dived on the Messerschmitts from behind. Flight Lieutenant C J Mount was leading the squadron and, in the initial attack and the subsequent chase when the 109s turned tail, they claimed eight of the German fighters. The day's losses were 19 German to seven British.

The 30 October saw more fighter-versus-fighter actions, but overall activity was much reduced and it was not until late morning that the first plots appeared on the British radar screens. Ten RAF squadrons were on their patrol lines, and six sighted the raiding aircraft. Two Bf 109s were shot down but 222 Squadron up from Hornchurch lost two pilots and a Spitfire was damaged. In the afternoon 130 Bf 109s streamed in across the south coast, and some reached London. Half a dozen were shot down but the RAF lost four aircraft,

LEFT: *The remarkable Squadron Leader Douglas Bader served with No 242 Squadron during the Battle of Britain.*

and 602 Squadron which had scored so well the previous day lost two Spitfires. On the 31st air activity was practically nil. The Luftwaffe lost 325 aircraft during October. The RAF lost 100 pilots with a further 85 wounded. It had been indeed a dangerous sky.

It was now evident to everyone that the battle was over. The raids were greatly reduced, the bombers were few and far between and with the coming of winter the Germans could no longer maintain an offensive in daylight. In any case they had been so badly mauled that they could not make an effective assault except by raiding at night. The accepted casualty figures for the Battle of Britain, the first major battle fought solely in the air, and which officially lasted from 10 July to 31 October 1940 are:

Luftwaffe aircraft lost	1733
German aircrew lost	3089
RAF fighters lost	915
RAF aircrew lost	503

Claims by both sides were exaggerated at the time, the RAF claimed to have shot down 2698 German aircraft, the Germans claimed 3058 RAF machines.

Undoubtedly the chief architect of the victory gained by Fighter Command was its Commander in Chief, Air Chief Marshal Hugh Dowding. His control was faultless. His foresight in designing and building his air-defense system saved Britain in its darkest hour. Laurels too must go to Air Vice-Marshal Keith Park who had so ably commanded 11 Group which daily took the brunt of the assault. He commanded his squadrons with remarkable insight and courage.

Despite the victory, there was little respite for the pilots of Fighter Command. November continued to see the fighters meeting in combat over southern England.

No 145 Squadron got itself into a tight spot on 7 November near the Isle of Wight. On patrol it was surrounded by three large formations of Bf 109s – totaling about 50. The Hurricane pilots were unable to engage or dive away without exposing themselves to attack but

RIGHT: *Flying Officer D Ward of No 87 Squadron. A New Zealander, he carried an unusual crest on his Hurricane, depicting a number of 'bad luck' charms – a broken mirror, lighting three cigarettes with one match, walking under a ladder and the number 13. His luck ran out in June 1942 when he was killed in North Africa.*

the Bf 109s began to pick off the members of B Flight. Five were hit and sent down and one pilot, Pilot Officer A N C Weir, DFC, was killed.

Four days later came the famous action when the Italians raided in the locality of Harwich. Nos 17, 46 and 257 Squadrons were in the air. Flight Lieutenant H P Blatchford, leading 257 Squadron, gained fame by destroying one Fiat BR 20 bomber and probably a Fiat CR 42 fighter biplane which he hit with his propeller.

The Italians were to make only a few intrusions over England in 1940. Another raid occurred on 23 November. No 603 Squadron found them and gave the call that it had spotted the ancient-looking machines. Another squadron in the area asked where they could be found. Perhaps an indication of the vast numbers and caliber of the enemy the pilots of 603 Squadron had been used to engaging was their classic reply:

'Shan't tell you, we're only outnumbered three to one!'

They shot down several of them. Before this, however, another veteran, Flying Officer M B Czernin, DFC, of 17 Squadron, was shot down. On the 17th he attacked a formation of Bf 110s of EG210, hit one but was then shot down by the famed Adolf Galland. Count Czernin baled out successfully. Flight Lieutenant Blatchford, again leading 257 Squadron shot down a Bf 109 on the same day after a bit of a chase. The Bf 109 pilot shot down a Hurricane during the fight but Blatchford finally nailed him:

'He continued to dive and I followed behind and above. After 30 seconds when at about 1500 feet, he flattened out and I put the finishing touches on him. The EA did a cartwheel and the pilot was jettisoned into the sea, pilot and aircraft hitting the sea at the same time 30 yards apart.'

The dangers in the sky continued to the end of the month. On the 28th came the now famous action when Flight Lieutenant J C Dundas, DFC, was lost near the Isle of Wight after possibly shooting down one of the leading German pilots, Helmut Wick of JG2. Dundas died with the yell of victory on his lips. In the air too was 152 Squadron, which was attacked by Bf 109s which screamed through its formation, shooting down veteran flier Pilot Officer A R Watson who had flown all through the battle. He baled out but tore his parachute in doing so and fell to his death. Pilot Officer E S Marrs went after the yellow-nosed Bf 109:

'I followed and caught it up about 10,000 feet at about 10 to 15 miles south of the Needles. I waited my time and closed to about 100 yards. EA was not turning or weaving at all and evidently did not suspect any pursuit. I gave a short burst from astern and slightly underneath and oil smothered over my windscreen. EA did a half roll and dived down. I broke away . . . and when I saw it again, pilot was floating down by parachute. EA machine was descending in flaming fragments, evidently exploded.'

Each summer we remember and recall with pride that summer of 1940 when a handful of gallant young men daily carried out feats of great valor above southern England. Many died in the battle, others were to die before the war finally ended nearly five years later. As we watch the fast jet fighter aircraft of today we know that the spirit which the 1940 pilots engendered then still lives on in the men who fly above us today. Churchill's famous 'Few' gave of their best then. Let us hope that the men of today never have to show the world again what an air war can mean.

ABOVE, FAR LEFT: *Three Hurricanes come in to land after a successful encounter with a formation of Italian aircraft, November 1940.*

ABOVE LEFT: *Flight Lieutenant J Dundas, DFC, downed Luftwaffe ace Helmut Wick (above) of JG2 on 28 November, but fell victim to the guns of one of Wick's comrades.*

ABOVE RIGHT: *Helmut Wick's Bf 109. Note the 42 victory bars on the tailfin.*

RIGHT: *Smiling members of No 41 Squadron, including Squadron Leader D Finlay, DFC, in the center.*

LEFT: *Messerschmitt Bf 109E, 'Red 13,' shot down over Sussex on 25 October. Its pilot was taken prisoner by a local farmer. The Battle of Britain officially ended on the 31st. The Luftwaffe had lost 1733 aircraft; the RAF 915.*

APPENDIX

Luftwaffe aircrew casualties

Bomber crews	1176
Stuka crews	85
Fighter-bomber crews	212
Fighter crews	171
Crewmen missing	1445
	3089

RAF fighter bases during the Battle of Britain, in Fighter Command's three main Fighter Groups.
(Names marked with an asterisk denote Sector Headquarters.)

10 Group HQ at Rudloe Manor, Box, Wiltshire.

Pembrey*	Bibury
Filton*	Colerne
Exeter	St Eval*
Roborough	Boscombe Down
Middle Wallop*	Aston Down
Warmwell	Sutton Bridge
Hawarden	

11 Group HQ at Hillingdon House, Uxbridge, Middx.

Debden*	Biggin Hill*
Castle Camps	Gravesend
Martlesham Heath	Redhill
North Weald*	Hawkinge
Stapleford	Lympne
Hornchurch*	Tangmere*
Rochford	Westhampnett
Manston	Ford
Kenley*	Northolt*
Croydon	Hendon
West Malling	

12 Group HQ at Watnall, Nottingham, Notts.

Duxford*	Speke
Coltishall*	Ringway
Wittering*	Church Fenton*
Digby*	Leconfield
Kirton-in-Lindsey*	Yeadon

Aircrew who took part in Battle of Britain

	Total	Killed
British RAF personnel	2384	398
Fleet Air Arm	57	9
Australians	21	13
New Zealanders	100	11
Canadians	87	20
South Africans	21	9
Rhodesians	2	–
Jamaicans	1	–
Irish	9	–
Americans	7	1
Poles	135	29
Czechs	85	8
Belgians	27	5
Israelis	1	–
French	12	–
	2949	503

Squadrons, flights and other units which took part in the Battle of Britain.

Sqdn No	Aircraft	Sqdn No	Aircraft	Sqdn No	Aircraft
1	Hurricane	92	Spitfire	264	Defiant
1 RCAF	Hurricane	111	Hurricane	266	Spitfire
3	Hurricane	141	Defiant	302	Hurricane
17	Hurricane	145	Hurricane	303	Hurricane
19	Spitfire	151	Hurricane	310	Hurricane
23	Blenheim	152	Spitfire	312	Hurricane
25	Blenheim	213	Hurricane	501	Hurricane
29	Blenheim	219	Blenheim	504	Hurricane
32	Hurricane	222	Spitfire	600	Blenheim
41	Spitfire	229	Hurricane	601	Hurricane
43	Hurricane	232	Hurricane	602	Spitfire
46	Hurricane	234	Spitfire	603	Spitfire
54	Spitfire	235	Blenheim	604	Blenheim
56	Hurricane	236	Blenheim	605	Hurricane
64	Spitfire	238	Hurricane	607	Hurricane
65	Spitfire	242	Hurricane	609	Spitfire
66	Spitfire	245	Hurricane	610	Spitfire
72	Spitfire	247	Gladiator	611	Spitfire
73	Hurricane	248	Blenheim	615	Hurricane
74	Spitfire	249	Hurricane	616	Spitfire
79	Hurricane	253	Hurricane	421 Flight	Hurricane
85	Hurricane	257	Hurricane	F.I.U.	Blenheim
87	Hurricane	263	Hurricane		

Main Luftwaffe units which took part in the Battle of Britain.

Kampfgeschwader 1	Heinkel 111 and Dornier 17
Kampfgeschwader 2	Dornier 17
Kampfgeschwader 3	Dornier 17
Kampfgeschwader 4	Heinkel 111 and Junkers 88
Kampfgeschwader 26	Heinkel 111
Kampfgeschwader 27	Heinkel 111
Kampfgeschwader 30	Junkers 88
Kampfgeschwader 51	Junkers 88
Kampfgeschwader 53	Heinkel 111
Kampfgeschwader 54	Junkers 88
Kampfgeschwader 55	Heinkel 111
Kampfgeschwader 76	Dornier 17
Kampfgeschwader 77	Junkers 88
Lehrgeschwader 1	Junkers 88, Junkers 87 and Messerschmitt 110
Lehrgeschwader 2	Messerschmitt 109 and 110
Stukageschwader 1	Junkers 87
Stukageschwader 2	Junkers 87
Stukageschwader 3	Junkers 87
Stukageschwader 51	Junkers 87
Stukageschwader 77	Junkers 87
Zerstörergeschwader 2	Messerschmitt 110
Zerstörergeschwader 26	Messerschmitt 110
Zerstörergeschwader 76	Messerschmitt 110
Erprobungsgruppe 210	Messerschmitt 110 and 109
Jagdgeschwader 2	Messerschmitt 109
Jagdgeschwader 3	Messerschmitt 109
Jagdgeschwader 26	Messerschmitt 109
Jagdgeschwader 27	Messerschmitt 109
Jagdgeschwader 51	Messerschmitt 109
Jagdgeschwader 52	Messerschmitt 109
Jagdgeschwader 53	Messerschmitt 109
Jagdgeschwader 54	Messerschmitt 109
Jagdgeschwader 77	Messerschmitt 109

Plus various reconnaissance, air-sea-rescue, coastal and night intruder units.

INDEX

Page numbers in *italics* refer to illustrations.

ACKNOWLEDGMENTS

The author and publishers would like to thank Martin Bristow for designing this book and Moira Dykes for the picture research. The following agencies and individuals provided photographic material:

Bison Picture Library: 9(top), 1˝(below), 20-21, 22, 27(below), 34, 36(below), 39(top), 42(both), 43(all 3), 45(below left), 46(top), 47(top right & below), 66(both), 67(top), 70, 74(top 2), 75(top).
Chaz Bowyer: 12(top), 13(below), 14(below), 15(below), 16(both), 17(top), 23(top), 24(top), 26(both), 27(top), 28, 31, 32(top), 36(top), 40(below), 41(below), 44(both), 45(below right), 46(below), 48(below), 49(top & below right), 50, 51(top), 55(top), 57(below), 58(top), 61(below), 64, 67(below), 68(below), 69(both), 73(both), 76(top left & below)/**Imperial War Museum:** 10(top), 11(both), 13(top), 19(below).

Bundesarchiv: 10(below), 18(top).
Norman Franks: 24(below), 25(both), 29, 33, 45(top), 48(top), 51(below right), 68(top), 75(below), 77(all 3)/**Imperial War Museum:** 40(top), 49(below right), 76(top right)/**Ministry of Defence:** 23(below).
Archiv Gerstenberg: 15(top).
M.J. Hooks: 6-7, 47(top left).
Robert Hunt Picture Library: 5, 18(below), 37, 58(below), 63(below).
Imperial War Museum: 2-3, 8, 9(below), 12(below), 14(top), 19(top), 30(both), 32(below), 41(top), 51(below left), 52-53, 54(top), 55(below), 56, 59(top right & below), 62(both), 63(top), 72, 74(below).
Museum of London: 60.
RAF Museum: 39(below).
T.R.H./RAF Museum: 54(below), 57(top), 59(top left), 61(top).